Oh, for an Onion!

Stapleford '90

Oh, for an Onion!

Denise Greig

Kangaroo Press

For Oden Greig, with love

Illustrations by Jane Stapleford

First published in 1990 by Kangaroo Press Pty Ltd
3 Whitehall Road (P.O. Box 75) Kenthurst NSW 2156
Typeset by G.T. Setters Pty Limited
Printed in Singapore by Kyodo Printing Co (S'pore) Pte Ltd

ISBN 0 86417 282 6

Contents

Introduction

Without the onion there would be no gastronomic art. Banish it from the kitchen and all pleasure of eating flies with it . . . its absence reduces the rarest dainty to insipidity, and the diner to despair.

[Anon]

And indeed where would we be without the onion? It is the most commonly used flavouring vegetable in the world today and has been around for about 6000 years. It is the vegetable that is the most taken for granted but without it we would miss out on some important health factors. We use onions every day, but only ever talk about them when some natural disaster causes their price to sky-rocket.

The onion counts among its close relatives garlic, chives, leeks, shallots and Japanese bunching onions. All edible members of the onion family are mentioned in this book. Each chapter includes origin, history and gossip as well as the nutritional and curative properties of these plants. There is a selection of classic recipes such as French onion soup, pickled onions, vichyssoise, cock-a-leekie, beurre blanc, aioli, garlic bread and garlic prawns as well as tempting new ideas on how to serve your favourite onion.

The onion and its pungent cousins are not only flavoursome additions to our diet, but are so easy to grow they will thrive almost anywhere. For onion lovers everywhere and gardeners alike there is a chapter devoted to their cultivation. Garlic and onions are well-known insecticides and included are recipes which will repel several unwanted insect pests in the garden.

The genus *Allium*

The genus *Allium* was for a long time included as a member of the Lily family, Liliaceae. Some botanists classed it as a member of the Amaryllis family, Amaryllidaceae, but it is now generally agreed to be treated as a separate family, Alliaceae.

The genus *Allium* itself is large in both number of species and area of distribution. Perhaps as many as 450 species are known, native primarily to the northern hemisphere. Some are grown as ornamentals; others are noxious weeds. But the best known species are those hardy plants cultivated in the vegetable garden for their edible bulbs and sometimes for their leaves, which are used in seasoning.

What distinguishes the alliums is the pungency of the leaves and bulbs. Most have an underground storage system, such as a bulb or tuber. The leaves may be basal or may clothe the stem higher up in a succession of tubular sheaths. The inflorescence is an umbel and the six segments of the perianth are usually petal-like. The seeds are most often black and rather angular, but are sometimes long, slender and flat. Much less frequently the seeds are almost round.

The Universal Onion

If there is one vegetable which is universal in its appeal, it is the onion *(Allium cepa)*. It is the most commonly used flavouring vegetable in the world and is relished for its pungent, individual taste. For over 6000 years onions have been used by man and they reach our table in some form every day.

The onion has been cultivated for so long that it is difficult to trace its origin, but it is believed to have been grown in India, China and the Middle East from prehistoric times and it probably originated around Iran and West Pakistan.

Onions were a well-known garden vegetable in Egypt: evidence from tombs dates back to the first and second dynasties (c.3200 – c.2780 BC). The onion is to be found sculptured on ancient Egyptian monuments, and it had a place in the worship and daily lives of the people. Onions formed the staple diet of the pyramid labourers and, together with garlic, was used to prevent sickness and fatigue.

The Israelites thought so highly of the onion, the leek and garlic that they cultivated them in Palestine after the Exodus (c.1500 BC).

The cultivation of the onion spread to India in about 600 BC. The Romans introduced the onion to Britain and throughout western Europe. They were used as currency in the Middle Ages. Later the Spanish took the onion to the West Indies and from there it spread to all parts of the Americas. However the American Indians were already using a highly pungent wild onion *(Allium canadense)* to flavour their food.

Onions and health

Onions are supposed to be the secret of good health and many curative powers have been attributed to them throughout the centuries. They have been used to lower blood sugar; to stimulate the heart; to eliminate fat; to stimulate the production of bile and urine; as well as to combat colds and viral infections.

The use of onions for the bacteria-destroying power of their vapour was demonstrated on a large scale in World War II. However this antibacterial action was found to be present only when the onion was freshly cut. The power disappeared within ten minutes.

Onions contain vitamins B and C. They also contain protein, iron, carbohydrate and natural sugar. The green tops have a high vitamin A content.

Onion varieties

Onions vary enormously in shape, size, flesh colour, texture and intensity of flavour. The shape may be oval, globe or slightly flattened. The bulb consists of a number of fleshy layers covered with a few dry skins. The outer layers may contain pigments that produce red, purple, yellow or variegated tints.. These pigments are usually absent in white onions. The onion contains a great deal of sugar and a characteristic volatile oil that produces the typical onion flavour. Depending on the composition of this oil, varieties are sweet, mild or pungent in taste.

Globe-shaped onions with yellow-brown skins have a cream-coloured flesh and a strong pungent flavour. They are medium to large in size and are used mainly in soups, casseroles and other cooked dishes. They are a staple in most kitchens.

The white round onions with dry white papery skins have a sharp medium flavour. The size varies from quite large to small which can be used for pickling. They are often cooked and may be stuffed, roasted or fried. These are the onions most often used in Asian cooking. They are also used raw and sliced for salads and as a garnish, but must be used sparingly.

Red onions are usually large, sweet and juicy. The flavour is mild and sweet. Their size makes them suitable for stuffing and baking. They make good fried onions and can be used raw in salads or sliced as a garnish.

Spring onions are small white onions that are sold fresh in bunches with long hollow leaves. They have a mild onion flavour. They are used whole in cooking and are often served raw in salads. Spring onions are also used for pickling.

Onions in the kitchen

Onions are available all year round. Choose onions that are firm, with a dry outer skin that is smooth and shiny. Avoid any that have begun to sprout and never buy onions that feel soft or wet, or smell musty. Onions deteriorate rapidly once the outer skin is removed and should not be stored after peeling and cutting.

Onions are used as a flavouring or as a delicious vegetable in their own right. They may be baked, boiled, braised, fried, sautéed or eaten raw. Large ones may be stuffed.

When peeling onions, a sulphur-rich volatile oil is released which causes the eyes to water. Tears can be avoided by peeling onions under running cold water to reduce the vapour in the air. To peel a large number of small onions, place in a bowl and pour on boiling water. Leave for a minute or two and drain. Skins will slip off easily.

Slice, chop or grate onions according to need. When sautéeing onions, slice evenly to ensure slices cook golden at the same time. As a garnish, separate paper-thin onion slices into rings.

Deep-fried onion rings

4 medium onions
1 cup milk
seasoned plain flour
oil

Cut onions into 1 cm slices. Separate into rings and sprinkle with milk. Leave for 30 minutes. Drain well then dust with flour. Fry a few at a time in deep oil for 2 or 4 minutes or until light golden brown. Drain on absorbent paper. Serve immediately.

Glazed white onions

A delicious vegetable dish that goes particuarly well with chicken, veal or fish.

20 small white onions, peeled
½ cup chicken stock
2 tablespoons butter
salt and freshly ground black pepper
2 tablespoons parsley, finely chopped

Bring the chicken stock and the butter to the boil in a large heavy frying pan. Season with a little salt and pepper. Add the onions and move them about until they are well coated. Cook uncovered over a low heat for about 30 minutes until the onions are tender and the liquid has reduced to a syrupy glaze. If necessary remove the onions and reduce the liquid further. Sprinkle with parsley and serve in a heated vegetable dish. Serves 4.

Spanish Onion Salad

3 red Spanish onions, sliced thinly
3 tablespoons olive oil
2 tablespoons vinegar
1 tablespoon lemon juice
3 tablespoons finely chopped parsley
salt and freshly ground black pepper

Cover thinly sliced onion rings with vinegar and allow to marinate for at least 1 hour. Drain. Mix lemon juice with oil and season with a little salt and black pepper. Pour over onions and toss well. Sprinkle with parsley before serving. Serves 4 as a side dish.

Pickled Onions

1 kg small white onions
10 cups water
2 cups salt
4 cups vinegar
¼ cup brown sugar
1 tablespoons black peppercorns
2 teaspoons whole allspice
2 whole cloves
small hot red chillies

Cover onions with boiling water. Let stand for a few minutes. Drain and rinse with cold water. Remove outer skins. Soak onions for 48 hours in brine made with the cold water and salt. Cover with a plate to ensure that all onions are totally immersed.

Drain and wash onions well before packing into sterilised jars. Bring to the boil the vinegar, sugar, pepper, allspice and cloves. Simmer over low heat for 5 minutes. Strain vinegar over the onions, filling the jar to well cover the onions. Add a red chilli to each jar. Seal and leave for 2 to 3 months before using.

Onion and Garlic Relish

This delicious relish is perfect with cold meats and is a good summer holiday standby as it can be kept in a covered jar in the refrigerator for up to 4 weeks.

1 kg brown onions, finely chopped
10 cloves garlic, crushed
½ cup olive oil
½ teaspoon allspice
1 tablespoon lime juice

13

Heat olive oil gently in a heavy saucepan. Add onions, garlic and allspice. Stir over a medium heat until slightly browned. Reduce heat, cover pan and cook very gently for 1 hour, stirring occasionally. Add lime juice. Pour into sterilised jars. Seal when cold and refrigerate until required.

Glazed Onions with Sherry

500 g small white onions, peeled
2 tablespoons butter
1 tablespoon brown sugar
⅓ cup dry sherry
½ cup water
salt and pepper

Heat butter in heavy frying pan. Add onions and sauté over a medium heat for a few minutes, turning occasionally. Add sugar and a little salt and pepper, stirring until sugar has melted. Add sherry and water, stir well. Reduce heat and continue cooking without a lid until the liquid has almost evaporated and onions are glazed. Serves 4.

Baked Stuffed Onions

6 medium to large onions, peeled

Filling
½ cup finely chopped ham or bacon
2 tablespoons butter
½ cup mushrooms, finely chopped
2 tablespoons soft white breadcrumbs
2 tablespoons cream
1 teaspoon marjoram, finely chopped
salt and freshly ground black pepper

Topping
butter
freshly grated parmesan cheese

Place onions in boiling salted water and simmer for 10 minutes. Drain and cool slightly. Cut off tops and scoop out centres carefully with a teaspoon, leaving 3 layers of flesh. Chop scooped-out centres to make 2 tablespoons chopped onions.

Melt butter in saucepan and sauté ham and mushrooms until soft. Add breadcrumbs, cream, marjoram and a little salt and pepper. Mix the stuffing well and spoon filling into onions. Place on a greased baking dish, sprinkle with grated parmesan and place a dot of butter on each. Bake at 200°C for 30 minutes. Serves 6.

Onions Stuffed with Garlic

6 medium to large onions

Filling
12 cloves garlic
1 tablespoon olive oil
2 tablespoons soft white breadcrumbs
6 tablespoons parsley, finely chopped
salt and freshly ground black pepper

Topping
extra breadcrumbs and butter

Place onions and garlic in boiling salted water and simmer for 10 minutes. Cut off tops and carefully scoop out centres of onions. Chop centres of onions and finely chop garlic. Place in a bowl and beat in olive oil, breadcrumbs, parsley, salt and pepper until mixture forms a smooth paste. Spoon filling into onions. Place on a greased baking dish, sprinkle with breadcrumbs and place a dot of butter on each. Bake at 200°C for 30 minutes, or until cooked through. Serves 6.

Sage and Onion Sauce

A rich brown sauce traditionally served with roast pork or duck. To enrich the flavour add two tablespoons of the meat juices from the baking dish to the sauce before serving.

2 medium onions, finely chopped
2 tablespoons butter
1 ½ cups brown stock
1 teaspoon sage leaves, finely chopped
2 tablespoons soft brown breadcrumbs
salt and freshly ground black pepper

Cook finely chopped onions in the butter over a low heat until a light brown colour. Add stock and stir until the mixture comes to boiling point. Add sage, breadcrumbs and season with a little salt and pepper. Stir in meat juices and serve separately.

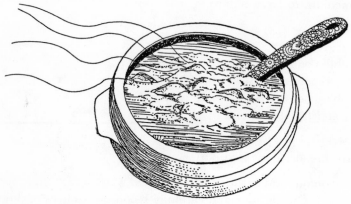

French Onion Soup

The onions for an onion soup need patient, slow cooking in butter for them to develop a rich golden brown colour. This preliminary process cannot be rushed and needs constant attention.

750 g onions, thinly sliced
4 tablespoons butter
1 teaspoon sugar
6 cups beef stock
100 ml cognac
salt and freshly ground black pepper
6 slices French bread
gruyere cheese, grated

Sweet and sour onions

Vichyssoise

18

Heat butter in a large heavy saucepan with the sugar. Add onions and cook slowly, stirring frequently, until the onions are a rich golden brown. This will take about 20 minutes. Stir in the beef stock gradually and bring to the boil. Lower the heat, cover and simmer gently for 45 minutes. Just before serving, stir in the cognac and season with salt and pepper. Pour into individual heatproof bowls. Place in each bowl of soup a slice of French bread heaped with grated cheese. Place in a very hot oven or under a pre-heated grill until cheese is melted and golden. Serve immediately. Serves 6.

Onion Tart

750 g onions, sliced
2 eggs, beaten
¾ cup grated gruyere cheese
salt and freshly ground black pepper

Shortcrust Pastry
225 g plain flour
125 g butter
2 tablespoons water
pinch of salt

Sift flour and salt into bowl. Rub in butter until mixture resembles breadcrumbs. Add water gradually, mixing to a firm dough. Place onto a floured board and knead very lightly until smooth. Chill for 30 minutes while preparing the onions.

Melt butter in a heavy saucepan and stir in onions. Over a very low heat, cover and cook onions gently for about 30 minutes. Remove from heat and stir in beaten eggs and grated cheese. Roll out pastry to line base of 25 cm flan tin. Fill with onion mixture and bake in a moderate oven for about 30 minutes.

Tomato and Onion Pasta Sauce

1 kg ripe tomatoes, peeled and diced
6 onions, chopped finely
90 g butter
salt and freshly ground black pepper

Melt butter in large frying pan with a lid. Sauté onions, then cover and turn heat to low. Cook onions for about 20 minutes until a pale golden colour. Do not allow to brown. Add diced tomatoes and sauté over a high heat for about 5 minutes. Season with salt and a few twists of the pepper grinder. The tomatoes should retain some of their identity and should not reduce to a pulp. Serve with pasta and freshly grated parmesan cheese.

Baked Onions

Onions are a great addition to the family roast and can be peeled and added to the roasting pan during the last 45 to 60 minutes of cooking. Turn them over once or twice during cooking and baste with the juices of the roast. The onions should be tender and golden but still in good shape.

Unpeeled Baked Onions

Place medium-sized onions, unpeeled, upright on a lightly buttered baking dish. Bake for about 1½ hours in a moderate oven. Large onions may take longer. When they are ready they will be soft to the touch. Cut a slice from the root end and the skins will slip off easily. Serve with salt, pepper and butter.

Sweet and Sour Onions

This dish is a perfect accompaniment to grilled meat, poultry and roasts. It can also be served cold as a relish and is wonderful with cold meats and salads.

1 kg small pickling onions, peeled

4 tablespoons olive oil
1 cup water
½ cup dry white wine
4 tablespoons lemon juice
100 g sultanas
2 tablespoons tomato paste
2 bay leaves
½ teaspoon thyme, chopped
salt and freshly ground black pepper
parsley, finely chopped

Place onions in a saucepan with all the ingredients and bring to the boil, stirring. Reduce heat, cover and simmer slowly for about 1 hour or until the onions are tender, but still holding their shape. The sauce should have reduced to a syrup. If not, remove the lid and boil down at the end of cooking. Transfer to a dish and allow to cool. Serve sprinkled with finely chopped parsley. Serves 6 as a side dish.

Barbecued Onions

4 flat Spanish onions
4 tablespoons olive oil
salt
freshly ground black pepper

Peel dry outer skin from onions, but do not remove the root or the tip. Cut in half horizontally. Place the onions on the barbecue flat sides down. When the sides facing the heat have charred, turn them over, making sure that all the rings are intact. Dress each onion with a tablespoon of oil and a sprinkling of salt. Move to the side of the barbecue with less heat and allow to cook a little more while the rest of the barbecue is cooking. When ready to serve, remove the charred outer skin and cut the onion into quarters. Season with a little salt and freshly ground black pepper. The onion should still be a little crunchy, but without any trace of pungency. Serves 4 as part of a meal.

Good Garlic

Treasured by many as a flavouring, garlic has been considered a healthy bulbous herb from the beginning of civilisation. It has been cultivated for at least 5000 years and, next to the onion, is the most widely cultivated *Allium*.

Garlic *(Allium sativum)* as we know it is a cultivar and is not known as a wild plant. It is of such antiquity that it is difficult with any certainty to trace the country of its origin, although many pens point to Central Asia where it is thought to have derived from its wild ancestor *A. longicuspis*. It has been around for millennia in countries bordering on the Mediterranean, and is used so lavishly that it is sometimes referred to as *la vanille de Marseille*. Garlic has always been a basic Chinese condiment and was recorded in a medical treatise in India around 6 BC.

Ancient Egyptians grew it together with leeks, onions, cucumbers and radishes. It was believed garlic had strength-giving properties and along with onions and radishes was the food of the labourers who built the pyramids. Dried bulbs of garlic, perfectly preserved, were found in the tomb of Tutankhamen, 1361–1352 BC, dating from around 1300 BC.

The ancient Greeks pressed the juice from garlic and drank great quantities while training and before games. It was a common item of diet and renowned for giving health and energy. Theophrastus (370–287 BC), who succeeded Aristotle as head of the Lyceum, tell us the Greeks used to place garlic on piles of stones at crossroads as a supper for Hecate, the goddess of witchcraft and sorcery.

Roman labourers and warriors consumed large quantities of garlic and it was recommended as a medicine by Dioscorides, chief doctor of the Roman armies in the first century AD. The Romans spread garlic throughout western Europe and introduced it to England.

In the Middle Ages, garlic was considered a cure for leprosy, a plague preventive and a famous charm against vampires. In a French outbreak of plague, in 1722, four robbers who made a profession of robbing plague victims used a highly aromatic lotion containing garlic and several herbs and spices as a safeguard. This mixture became famous afterwards as the 'Four Thieves Vinegar'.

The Medicinal Garlic

Many of the old writers praised garlic as a medicine. Hippocrates (468–370 BC), the Father of Medicine, has many medicinal uses of garlic attributed to him. Both Pliny and Dioscorides mention garlic as a cure for dropsy, a disinfectant, an antiasthmatic and a cold cure. For centuries it has been regarded as an antidote to intestinal worms; both in early Roman days and in Chinese herbalism. Throughout time garlic has been applied to skin infections, bites and stings.

In the trenches of World War I, sphagnum moss was first sterilised, then impregnated with garlic juice and used to treat infected wounds; because of garlic's known antiseptic qualitites. It was also used for preventing and curing gastro-intestinal infections.

Modern scientific research has verified a number of its traditional attributes. The bulb contains allicin, which is a natural antibiotic as well as a fungicide. Garlic is especially rich in sulphur compounds; vitamins A, B and C; high levels of trace minerals; sugars; and other beneficial substances. It has a beneficial effect on the digestive system; aids intestinal function; can help control blood pressure; lower the level of serum cholesterol in the blood; and help against hardening of the arteries.

Garlic is a known remedy for cold infections, catarrh, bronchitis and influenza. Hospital research in Russia in 1972 reported considerable success in the use of garlic extract inhalation to treat cases of lung tuberculosis.

It is agreed upon by all that fresh garlic is the most effective in treatment. However excessive intake of raw garlic may cause irritation to the mouth, esophagus and stomach. Raw garlic can also cause contact dermatitis on the fingers and hands of some people if handled in very large quantities. Cooked garlic is not irritative, but must be first cut or crushed to have any medicinal properties.

Garlic Breath

Shakespeare wrote this of garlic: 'And, most dear actors, eat no onion, nor garlic, for we are to utter sweet breath'. This was spoken in *A Midsummer Night's Dream* by Bottom to his fellow actors. Perhaps this was the start of garlic's bad name for bad breath among English-speaking people. Many people can't tolerate the smell of garlic on other people's breath and some immoderate garlic eaters do seem to exude an unpleasant garlic smell from their whole body surface.

There is, however, evidence to suppose that breath only smells offensively of garlic when the digestion is faulty. It may well be that the odour on crowded, southern European buses can be blamed on a lack of washing and not on garlic. The good news is that garlic eaters never notice the smell of garlic either on themselves or on others. And with all the benefits and sheer pleasure of eating garlic you might as well be 'in for a penny, in for a pound', and at the same time help keep vampires at a distance!

Cooking garlic slowly or unpeeled avoids any pungency and does not contaminate the breath. The traditional antidote to garlic breath is to chew fresh parsley after eating garlic. Thyme, rosemary and the seeds of caraway, dill and fennel have also been recommended to mask the smell.

Garlic in the Kitchen

Garlic has a very long tradition as a food and as a culinary ingredient. It is almost universal in its application, and is such a versatile flavouring that it complements nearly all savoury dishes; especially those of the cuisines of Asia and the Mediterranean regions.

It is perhaps the most controversial addition to food. Some can't live without it, some hate it and some are allergic to it. The quantity used in cooking is a highly personal matter, although it should not be allowed to overwhelm delicate foods.

Always use fresh garlic. It is available throughout the year and is easy to store. Garlic extract and garlic powder are inferior and sometimes taste bitter. There are several varieties differing in size of bulb, pungency and skin colour. The two types most often found in the markets are the common white-skinned garlic, made up of about ten small cloves; and the elephant garlic which is a larger and a somewhat milder variety, but which is not superior to the classic garlic. Look for firm, well-shaped, plump cloves. Avoid bulbs that are soft or sprouting. Purchase in small amounts and keep in a cool, dry spot away from sunlight. Do not store in the refrigerator. Break off only those cloves needed. Once detached the cloves dry out.

The best way to peel a clove of garlic is to smack each clove lightly but firmly with the broad side of a knife. The pressure breaks the skin which can then be easily removed. Further crushing can be done with the back of a spoon or by finely chopping to a puree. A little salt added softens the bulb almost at once and makes crushing or chopping even easier.

For those who prefer just a subtle hint of garlic, half a clove can be used to rub the inside of a salad bowl and discarded. Unpeeled whole cloves simmered in a stew or soup will produce the mildest garlic flavour.

Garlic Bread

Garlic bread is a family favourite to be eaten at any time. It will give a lift to the simplest meal. Several sticks can be made at the same time, wrapped in foil and frozen for convenience. Do not sprinkle with parmesan cheese before freezing.

1 French bread stick
2 cloves garlic, crushed
125 g butter, softened
1 tablespoon parsley, finely chopped
parmesan cheese, freshly grated (optional)
Foil wrap

Slice the bread into 2 cm diagonal slices but don't cut right through. Leave the bottom crust undisturbed. Cream butter in a bowl and fold in garlic and parsley. Spread butter thickly on both sides of each slide of bread. Sprinkle with parmesan cheese. Wrap bread in a large sheet of foil. Place in a preheated over 200°C (400°F) for 10 minutes. Open the foil parcel at the top and leave for a further 5 minutes to crisp the top. Serve hot.

Garlic Prawns

This popular Spanish restaurant dish is full of flavour and easy to prepare. Serve with crusty bread for dipping. Use only green prawns.

175 g green medium prawns
2 cups olive oil
125 g butter
8 cloves garlic, crushed
2 small red chillies, finely chopped
1 tablespoon parsley, chopped
freshly ground black pepper

Shell prawns leaving tail shell intact, then devein. Divide oil, butter, garlic and chillies and place into 4 individual heatproof dishes. Place in moderate oven for about 10 minutes until butter has melted and oil is very hot.

Remove from oven and divide prawns between dishes. Return to oven for about 8 minutes or until prawns are cooked. Cooking time depends on prawn size. Sprinkle with chopped parsley and grind black pepper over each bowl before serving immediately. Serves 4.

Bagna Cauda

(Hot Dip for Raw Vegetables)
This very popular dip is of northern Italian origin and is renowned as a Piedmont speciality. In Piedmont the vegetable most popular for dipping is the cardoon. However those who do not have this wonderful edible thistle on hand can substitute almost any raw vegetable. Suitable raw vegetables are strips of fennel, carrot, spring onions, celery, capsicum, cucumbers, zucchini, whole button mushrooms, cherry tomatoes, and cauliflower and broccoli florets sliced in half.

5 cloves garlic, crushed
¾ cup olive oil
60 g unsalted butter
8 flat anchovy fillets, drained, rinsed and finely chopped

Choose a flame-proof dish that fits over a candle warmer or spirit lamp. A fondue dish is also suitable. On the stove melt the butter and oil over a low heat. Add the garlic and lightly cook, but do not let it brown. Add the chopped anchovies, stirring constantly for about ten minutes. Bring the dish to the table and keep hot over the flame. To eat, pick up a vegetable with the fingers and dip for a moment into the hot sauce. Serve with Italian bread.

Aioli

Aioli is a wonderful aromatic mayonnaise that comes to us from Provence. It is a great favourite in the south of France where it is served with the local garden vegetables and the abundance of nearby seafood. It provides a delicious sauce for an outdoor lunch party in a shady part of the garden. Serve very lightly cooked vegetables such as new potatoes, carrots, asparagus, and beans.

Cooked vegetables should be still quite firm. Raw vegetables might include cherry tomatoes, small zucchinis, sliced capsicums and button mushrooms. For seafood, consider serving cold whole baked snapper or cold poached trout. Shellfish might include cooked prawns, crab, lobster and steamed mussels. Hard-boiled eggs, sliced in two, are a fine addition. Serve with good crusty bread and be generous with fresh herbs.

You might also wish to utilise the sauce with cold meats and poultry. It works very well with left over Christmas fare and is delicious served with ham, boiled potatoes and a few crispy vegetables. Cold roasts might include pork, lamb, beef, turkey, duck or chicken.

2 egg yolks at room temperature
8 cloves garlic, crushed finely
300 ml olive oil
1 teaspoon Dijon-style mustard
1 tablespoon white breadcrumbs
a little milk
1 teaspoon lemon juice
salt and white pepper

Soak the breadcrumbs in a little milk for a few minutes, then squeeze dry. Place in bowl or mortar and vigorously mash the bread and garlic to a smooth paste using a pestle or wooden spoon. Beat in the egg yolks. Add a little salt, some white pepper and the mustard. When the mixture is thick and sticky, begin to beat in the olive oil a drop at a time and beat well. Continue to add oil at this rate until the sauce suddenly changes while you are beating and you'll see that it has started to thicken. Gradually increase the amount of oil and continue to beat all the time. Gradually season with the lemon juice. The sauce will be like a firm mayonnaise. You might find that you do not need all the oil, so stop adding it when you feel that the mayonnaise is right. Should the aioli separate, stir in a spoonful of boiling water.

The above amount will serve 4 to 6 people. If you need a larger quantity remember that the exact quantity of oil is determined by the number of egg yolks used.

Bourride

Bourride is a wonderful garlicky fish dish of Provence. It is a good one to know if you have a keen fisherman in the house and you've run out of ideas on what to do with a miscellany of fish. One of the main ingredients is aioli, of which part is blended into the broth to make it a smooth rich yellow sauce and the rest offered in a separate dish. A bourride contains a variety of white sea fish such as bream, snapper, perch, John Dory, whiting, etc. However one variety of fish will do. A few king prawns, yabbies, Balmain bugs, lobster, or mussels can also be included for a splash of colour or for special occasions, but are not necessary.

1 kg white fish on the bone or fillets cut into thick serving pieces
1 stick celery
3 egg yolks
1 quantity of aioli, see above
parsley, finely chopped
8–12 slices of French bread, toasted

Stock
1 kg fish heads, bones and trimmings
1 litre water
150 ml dry white wine
1 leek, white part, thinly sliced
1 teaspoon fennel seed
1 strip of orange peel
sprigs of thyme
parsley stalks

Make the stock by simmering the fish heads, and bones and trimmings with the water, wine, leek, herbs and orange peel for about 15 minutes. Then strain it.

Pour the stock into a pan, add the celery and season lightly. Add the fish, bring to the boil and simmer uncovered for 3 to 8 minutes, or until the fish is just firm to the touch. Watch the fish carefully as different kinds and thicknesses cook at different speeds. With a slotted spoon, transfer the pieces to a heated serving dish.

In another pan, whisk half the aioli with the 3 egg yolks and

300 ml of the hot fish stock until it just thickens. Cook over a very low heat, stirring until the sauce thickens. Do not let it come to the boil. Season with salt, pepper and lemon juice if needed. Pour the sauce over the fish in the serving dish, arrange the shellfish on top if you are including it, and sprinkle the parsley on top.

To serve, place two or three slices of toast in a soup dish and spoon some of the fish and sauce on top. Serve the remaining aioli separately. Serve with plain boiled potatoes. Serves 4 to 6.

Chicken with Garlic

The forty cloves of garlic included in this classic French recipe known as *Poulet au Quarante Gousses* might appear a little excessive. But try it. The flavour is absolutely wonderful and it is so simple to prepare.

1 whole chicken
40 cloves garlic, peeled
1 cup unsalted butter, melted
assorted herbs
seasoning

Stuff a handful of herbs such as tarragon, parsley, chervil, thyme, etc. into prepared chicken. Place into a lidded casserole with the peeled garlic, and a touch of salt and pepper. Pour the melted butter over the chicken and cover with a tightly fitting lid. Cook in moderate oven for about 1½ hours, or until the chicken is tender. Serve warm with crusty peasant bread and a mixed green salad. Serves 4 to 6.

Baked Garlic

This Bordelaise dish is one for the garlic extremist. Serve as an appetiser with lightly toasted country-style bread and a bossy red wine. Large heads of garlic are essential.

4 whole fresh garlic bulbs
unsalted butter

sprigs of fresh thyme
salt and pepper

Cut a flat base to the garlic bulbs and remove the outer papery
skins around the upper, thickest part. Gently prise the cloves from
one another a little, but do not allow the cloves to break from the
bulb. Place the garlic bulbs on a greased oven dish and smear
lavishly with softened butter. Sprinkle with a little salt and pepper
and surround with the sprigs of fresh thyme. Roast uncovered in
a mdoerate to hot oven for 30 minutes, basting with the butter from
time to time. Lower heat to moderate and cover. Continue cooking
for about 1½ hours. The garlic should be very tender. Serve each
person a whole head. The puree is squeezed from the jacketed garlic
and spread onto a slice of toast. Serves 4.

Peperonata

(Capsicum Casserole with Garlic)
This colourful Italian dish can be served as an accompaniment to
grilled meat, poultry or fish dishes. It is a great summer dish when
capsicums are plentiful and large quantities can be made and stored
in the refrigerator for up to a week. It can be served cold or gently
reheated. Green and yellow capsicums can also be used, but the
red variety keep their colour best. The following serves 4 to 6.

800 g red capsicums
200 g sliced onions
6 cloves garlic, crushed
500 g peeled and chopped tomatoes
150 ml olive oil

Remove seeds and stems from capsicum and cut into linear slices.
In a heavy saucepan with a lid, heat the oil and gently cook the
onions and garlic until soft. Add the capsicums, a little salt and
pepper and allow to gently stew for another 10 minutes. Add the
tomatoes. Cover and continue cooking until the capsicum is soft
and the tomatoes have formed a thickish sauce. You may need to
remove the lid for the final 5 minutes of cooking, to allow the juices
to reduce a little.

Beurre d'Escargots

(Snail Butter)
Without garlic there would be no snail butter and snails would be
very dull indeed. Snails can be bought in tins, with shells in a
separate packet. It is a good idea to have specially grooved snail
dishes so the shells do not topple over and spill their delicious juices.
Special tongs to hold the snails have a spring in the handle which
allow you to regulate the end to the size of the snail. Small, closely-
tined forks are used to remove the snail. Allow about a dozen of
snail per serving. The following quantity will serve 4.

400 g butter
4 or more cloves garlic, well crushed
2 tablespoons fresh parsley, finely chopped
pinch nutmeg
salt and freshly ground black pepper

Pound garlic, butter and parsley well together so that all ingredients
are evenly distributed. Season to taste with a little salt, pepper and
nutmeg. Place a dab of snail butter in each shell. Put one snail
in each shell and fill generously with the prepared butter. The snails
are then heated in the oven just long enough to make them piping
hot.

Persian Pickled Garlic

Serve as tangy nibbles with a robust wine and cheese or as part
of a plate of mixed appetisers. The skins can be left on before
pickling, but peeling as you eat can be messy and fiddly.

1 kg whole cloves garlic, peeled or unpeeled
1 tablespoon sea salt
1 tablespoon whole coriander seeds, lightly bruised
12 whole black peppercorns
2 or 3 chillies
sprig of tarragon or thyme
white wine vinegar

Place all the dry ingredients in one jar, or divide into two, then cover completely with the wine vinegar. Seal and allow to stand in a cool place for at least 2 weeks before using. This pickle will keep for a long time and improves with age.

Garlic Olives

1 kg green olives, drained and rinsed
10 cloves garlic, peeled and sliced
2 tablespoons whole coriander seeds, lightly bruised
3 sprigs thyme
olive oil

Place olives, garlic, coriander and thyme in a large glass jar and cover completely with olive oil. Allow to stand in a cool place for at least 2 weeks to allow the flavour to develop. The oil gains a wonderful strong garlic flavour that can be used for cooking or salads.

Garlic

Leek flowers

Chopped leeks

Lovely Leeks

The leek *(Allium porrum)* as we know it is a cultivar and is not found in the wild. It is believed to be derived from *A. ampeloprasum*, a native of the eastern Mediterranean region, North Africa and parts of the USSR. The cultivated leek may be recognised by its flat, closely overlapping leaves forming a cylindrical white stem and not a rounded bulb.

The Egyptians cultivated and ate leeks and the Greeks and Romans made them into soup. It was so esteemed by the Romans that Nero is said to have eaten large quantities regularly to help clear his voice and so earned the nickname 'porrophagus' or 'leek-throated'.

The Romans distributed the leek throughout western Europe and introduced it to the British Isles. It became the national emblem of Wales and is traditionally worn on St David's day. It commemorates a battle in AD 640 in which the Welsh, led by their King Cadwallader, defeated the Saxons by wearing leeks in their caps to distinguish themselves from the enemy.

Leeks in the Kitchen

The leek is highly esteemed in the art of cookery. It has a delicate, mild sweet flavour in contrast to the onion. In France leeks are so plentiful they are called 'the asparagus of the poor' and are often cooked and served as a vegetable. Leeks can be served in much the same manner as asparagus. They can be served as an accompanying vegetable simmered in either butter or wine. Leeks are also a popular addition to soups, notably the Scottish cock-a-leekie soup and the French potage parmentier; which turns into the famous vichyssoise when served chilled. Leeks contain iron and small amounts of other vitamins and minerals. They are available all year round with good supplies in winter, when they often make a much better buy than a tray of tired soup vegetables.

Young medium-sized leeks are the best to buy. The tops should be fresh and green with a fair amount intact. If leeks have been drastically trimmed, it might indicate old age and they may have formed a hard solid stalk in the middle which cannot be used. As it is mostly the white part that is eaten, choose leeks with a good proportion of white stem. They are best used promptly, but may be stored for a short time in the refrigerator. Do not wash until ready to use.

Cleaning Leeks

Leeks are brutes to clean. Most leeks on sale look clean but it is only the outside dirt that has been removed. During the growing period, the thickened stems are blanched by hilling soil around them. The soil becomes lodged between the leaves, therefore the leeks need to be thoroughly washed before cooking. Remove the root, green tops and outer layer. To ensure all particles of grit are removed it is advisable to halve the leek lengthwise and hold under cold running water. When a recipe calls for leeks sliced in rings, loosen the top part so that water can run right through the vegetable.

Potage Parmentier; Vichyssoise

(Leek and Potato Soup)
4 medium potatoes, peeled and diced
5 large leeks, white part only, sliced
1 medium onion, sliced
3 cups chicken stock
4 tablespoons butter
1 cup double cream
salt and pepper
finely cut fresh chives

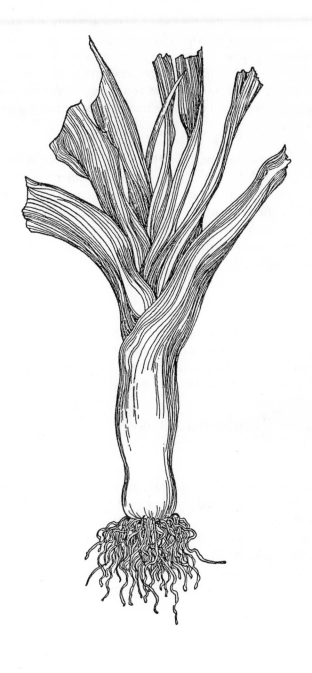

39

In a heavy saucepan sauté the leeks and onion gently in butter until soft. Do not allow to brown. Add to the leeks stock, potatoes and a little salt and pepper to taste, and simmer until the potatoes are well-cooked. Force the soup through a food mill or sieve into a bowl, and return to pan. Stir in the cream and bring to a simmer. Correct the seasoning. Serve in a tureen or individual soup bowls garnished with fresh chives.

Vichysoisse: In the summer of 1917 Louis Diat, chef at the Ritz-Carlton in New York City, devised a cold summertime version of Leek and Potato Soup that has since become famous the world over. To make it: after passing the potato and leek soup through a food mill, allow to cool. Stir in the double cream. Chill the soup until it is very cold. Serve sprinkled with finely-chopped chives. Serves 4 to 6.

Cock-a-Leekie

Cock-a-leekie is a warming soup from Scotland containing leeks and, sometimes, prunes. Some recipes for this soup include pearl barley and other thickening ingredients. This is not necessary and is not traditional; the addition of prunes is.

1 large chicken
10 large leeks, well washed and sliced
6 cups beef or strong chicken stock
250 g prunes, stoned

Remove excess fat from the bird and place in a very large saucepan. Cover with stock and bring slowly to the boil, skimming off any foam and scum. Add the leeks and simmer gently until the bird is almost cooked. Correct the seasoning and add the prunes for the last 20 minutes of cooking.

Remove the chicken to a plate, and joint. Place in a heated tureen and pour the remaining soup over. Serves 6.

Leeks au Gratin

12 leeks
4 tablespoons butter
4 tablespoons plain flour
1 ½ cups hot milk
125 g grated gruyere cheese
1 teaspoon mustard
2 tablespoons fresh breadcrumbs
a little salt and freshly ground black pepper

Cut off the roots of the leeks and most of the green leaves. Slice lengthways, stopping before reaching the root end, and wash thoroughly. Simmer gently in boiling salted water until just tender, then drain.

Melt butter in double saucepan. Blend in flour, stirring constantly until smooth. Add hot milk gradually, stirring until the sauce comes to the boil. Add cheese, stirring until the cheese melts. Season with mustard, lemon juice, salt and black pepper.

Lay the leeks in a buttered baking dish. Pour sauce over them and sprinkle with fresh breadcrumbs. Dot with some extra butter. Bake in moderate oven for about 20 minutes until golden brown and hot. Serves 4 to 6.

Cornish Leek Pie

6 leeks, washed and sliced
125 g bacon, diced
2 tablespoons butter
250 ml thickened cream
1 egg

Shortcrust Pastry

225 g plain flour
125 g butter
2 tablespoons water
pinch of salt

Sift flour and salt into bowl. Rub in butter until mixture resembles breadcrumbs. Add water gradually, mixing to a firm dough. Place onto a floured board and knead very lightly until smooth. Chill for 30 minutes before using.

Gently sauté leeks in the butter, cover and cook over low heat for 10 minutes. Remove from heat, add bacon. Grease an ovenproof pie plate (20–23 cm). Arrange leek and bacon mixture evenly on the bottom. Mix cream and egg well together and pour over the leek mixture. Roll out pastry and cover pie. Trim around edges and brush with milk. Bake for 30 minutes in a moderate oven or until the crust is golden brown. This pie is best eaten warm. Serves 4 to 6.

Leek and Tomato Salad

10 leeks, sliced thickly
5 medium tomatoes, peeled and cut in halves
12 black olives, stoned
2 tablespoons olive oil
juice of 1 lemon
2 teaspoons finely grated lemon peel
a little salt and freshly ground pepper
parsley, finely chopped

In a heavy saucepan heat oil and very gently sauté leeks. Add a dash of salt and pepper, cover and simmer for about 10 minutes. Add tomatoes, olives, lemon juice and peel, and cook slowly for a further 10 minutes. Allow to cool in the liquid and serve cold, garnished with chopped parsley. Serves 4 to 6 as a side dish.

Japanese Beef with Leeks

Dashi is an all-purpose seasoning used in almost every Japanese recipe. Instant dashi can be bought in packets at Asian food stores.

Ginger juice is made by squeezing freshly grated ginger through a cloth.

400 g lean rump steak, thinly sliced
3 leeks, white part sliced into rings
3 tablespoons sesame oil
1 cup dashi
⅓ cup soy sauce
⅓ cup mirin or medium dry sherry
2 tablespoons fresh ginger juice

Heat wok and when hot pour in the oil. Add the leeks and stir fry for 2 to 3 minutes. Add the beef slices and quickly stir until the meat loses its pink colour. Pour in the dashi, soy sauce and mirin and continue cooking for a further 2 minutes. Remove from heat and stir in the ginger juice. Serve immediately with boiled rice. Serves 4.

The True Shallot

Also known as eschallot in the USA and eschalote in France, the shallot *(Allium cepa* var. *ascalonium)*, should not be confused with Japanese bunching onions (which we call shallots in Australia). The common name madness has probably arisen because this species is often sold as green onions during spring and summer in the USA, and in many areas any green bunching onion is called a shallot, regardless of species.

Very little is known of the origin and background of this shallot, but it is often associated with the old Palestinian city of Ascalon and was supposedly introduced to Europe by returning Crusaders.

It is a small herbaceous plant to 45 cm high with cylindrical, hollow leaves tapering to a point. The pale lavender flowers, arranged in a compact umbel, are rarely produced. The bulbs are small, elongated or oval and are formed by several clusters of bulblets. Colour ranges from coppery yellow to reddish brown. The mature bulbs are used for flavouring or as small boiled onions.

Shallots are more expensive to buy than ordinary onions, but they are very easy to grow and multiply readily. Each clove produces ten or more new ones. They dry well and can be stored for months, making a good flavoursome standby. The larger bulbs do not always keep as well as the medium-sized ones.

True Shallots in the Kitchen

The flavour of the bulb is less pronounced than that of the onion and it is said to be easier to digest. Although it has much greater delicacy, it must be still used with discretion. The shallot has finely textured flesh and liquidises better than the onion, which is probably why it has earned the reputation of being the queen of the sauce onions. Of all the onion family, shallots are the most favoured in French cooking and are featured in sauces such as beurre blanc and marchand de vin. It is also used in salads or for a delicate, onion-like flavour in many dishes. Shallots also make great pickled onions.

The bulbs are eaten raw, boiled, baked or fried after removing the dry skin layers. Elongated varieties tend to be stronger-tasting. Shallots should never be browned as they become bitter. When sautéeing them, chop or mince fine so as not to subject them to too much heat.

Beurre Bercy
(Shallot Butter with White Wine)

A light and delicious sauce to serve with roast meat or fish. For the stock use juices from the roast or a little fish stock and a squeeze of lemon when serving with fish.

2 teaspoons finely chopped shallots
¾ cup dry white wine
2 tablespoons stock
¼ cup butter
2 teaspoons finely chopped parsley

Simmer shallots and wine until reduced by half original quantity. Add stock and correct seasoning. Remove from heat and stir through butter and parsley.

Beurre Marchand de Vin
(Shallot Butter with Red Wine)

Follow the preceding recipe, but substitute red wine for the dry white wine.

This butter is delicious served with sautéed liver. As soon as the liver has been removed to a dish, swirl the butter into the frying pan away from the heat. Pour over the liver and sprinkle with a little extra parsley.

Beurre Blanc
(White Butter Sauce)

This famous French sauce is said to have originated in Nantes on the Loire River and is traditionally served with pike, a freshwater fish. It goes well with just about all fish whether poached, steamed, baked or grilled; as well as shellfish. This sauce is just heaven served with lightly cooked asparagus and broccoli.

3 tablespoons white wine vinegar
3 tablespoons dry white wine
3 shallots, chopped almost to a puree
185 g unsalted butter, chilled and cut into about 12 pieces

Bring the vinegar, wine and shallots to the boil and cook, stirring occasionally until the liquid is reduced to about one tablespoon. Remove the saucepan from the heat and allow to cool a little. With a wire whisk beat in 2 pieces of butter. Beat in another piece of butter, whisking constantly until the liquid completely absorbs the butter. Return the saucepan to a very low heat and add the rest of the butter a piece at a time, whisking constantly and making sure that each lot has almost creamed into the sauce. At no time during cooking must the butter be allowed to completely melt or turn oily. The finished sauce must be frothy, thick and a pale cream colour. Immediately remove from heat as soon as all the butter has been used. Beat in a little salt and white pepper to taste if desired. Serve sauce at once. The rest of the food should be ready and waiting.

Blender Shallot Dressing

A quick and easy salad dressing perfect for mixed green salads and raw vegetables such as English spinach, sliced tomatoes and tiny whole mushrooms. It is also good on lightly cooked asparagus and snake beans cut into thirds.

⅓ cup white wine vinegar
¾ cup olive oil
2 tablespoons Dijon-style mustard
4 shallots, peeled
½ teaspoon salt
freshly ground black pepper

Place all ingredients in blender container and blend until smooth. Pour into bottle and store in refrigerator until required. Shake well before using. Makes 1 cup.

Shallots

What we call 'shallot' in Australia is not the true shallot but the Japanese bunching onion *(Allium fistulosum)*. In Britain it is also known as the Welsh onion, but has no association with Wales. The word 'Welsh' is in fact a corruption of the German *welsche*, meaning foreign.

Shallots are unknown in the wild state but were originally native to Eastern Asia. They have naturalised in south-central Norway, where they were used on turf roofs. Turf roofs were common all over Scandinavia and shallots were used as a protection from cows. The belief that shallots act as a protection against lightning may also have influenced their planting on turf roofs.

The Americans call them scallions and, to add to the confusion, many Asian cookbooks refer to them as spring onions. The difference between spring onions and bunching onions is that a bulb is formed on spring onions and the leaf in cross section is flattened. Shallots as we know them form long slender necks, rather than bulbs. The specific name refers to the hollow tube-like leaves, which are circular in cross-section.

As this book is written mostly with Australians in mind, I will continue to call them shallots. Also it would slow us down terribly and probably cause unnecessary communication problems if we asked for Japanese bunching onions at our favourite greengrocers. If you want the true shallot *(Allium cepa* var. *ascalonium)*, ask for the true or French shallot. I did, however, see bags of the true shallots being sold at the markets the other morning as 'red onions'!

It is fairly safe to assume that mention of spring onions, green onions or scallions in any Asian cookbooks written overseas refers to the shallots known to Australians. If shallot is mentioned as an ingredient in any overseas publication it will mean the true shallot.

Shallots in the Kitchen

Shallots have a mild, fresh onion flavour and are often added to some savoury dishes where onions would be too strong. Both the white bottoms and green tops are used as a lively addition to salads and as a garnish.

They are an essential ingredient in Japanese and Chinese cuisine and date back to the Han Dynasty, more than 2000 years ago. They are never served as a vegetable on their own, but often form part of a vegetable mixture. While the white root end is preferred in cooking, the green part is often shredded and used as a garnish. Remove the roots attached to the white end and peel the dry outer skin before using. Shallots may be minced, sliced in rounds, cut diagonally or shredded lengthways with a cleaver. When stir frying it is a good idea to have the white and green parts separate as the white part requires longer cooking. The green part is added at the end of cooking and swirled around at the last moment.

Fried Rice with Vegetables

4 cups short grain rice, cooked
2 eggs, beaten
½ cup sliced shallots, white part
2 stalks celery, diced
2 leeks, white parts sliced
2 carrots, diced
1 cup snake beans, sliced
4 dried Chinese mushrooms
4 tablespoons oil
1 teaspoon ginger, finely grated

2 cloves garlic, crushed
2 cups fresh bean sprouts
½ cup green part of shallots, sliced in rings
1 tablespoon oyster sauce
2 tablespoons soy sauce

The rice should be cold and is best cooked one day in advance. Flake the rice so that the grains do not stick together. Soak the mushrooms in a little hot water for 30 minutes. Pat dry, discard the stems and coarsely chop the caps. Heat a little oil in a wok and fry the beaten eggs, stirring them into pieces as they cook. Remove from wok and set aside. Place the wok over medium high heat and when it begins to smoke add the remaining oil. Add ginger and garlic and stir briefly. Add all the vegetables except the bean sprouts and green shallots, and quickly stir-fry for about 2 minutes. Stir in the rice, toss and fry over high heat until heated through. Pour in the oyster and soy sauce, tossing the rice over and over to blend everything. Stir in the bean sprouts, toss through and finally stir in the green parts of the shallots. Serve immediately. Serves 4 to 6 or more as a side dish.

Stir-Fried Bean Sprouts and Shallots

This very easy dish is rich in protein and requires only a very short cooking time. The bean sprouts need only to be heated through and should remain firm and crisp.

250 g fresh bean sprouts
8 shallots, sliced lengthways and cut into 2.5 cm lengths, white and
    green parts separated
1 teaspoon ginger, finely grated
2 cloves garlic, crushed
3 tablespoons oil
3 tablespoons soy sauce

Heat wok over a medium high heat and add the oil. When it is moderately hot add the white part of the shallots, garlic and ginger. Stir quickly for a minute. Stir in the bean sprouts and vigorously toss for about 2 minutes. Add soy sauce and stir and toss to mix. Finally add the green part of the shallots, toss and serve immediately. Serves 2 or more as part of a meal.

Variation: 225 g fresh Chinese noodles, lightly cooked in boiling water for a minute or two, can be tossed through the bean sprouts and shallots at the last moment for an appetising bowl of noodles. Serves 4.

Chicken Salad

2 whole chicken breasts, cooked
½ lettuce, shredded
6 shallots, julienned and retaining most of green
¼ cup fresh coriander leaves

Dressing

2 tablespoons hoisin sauce
2 tablespoons lemon juice
3 tablespoons oil
1 teaspoon sesame oil
1 tablespoons almond slivers, toasted, to garnish

Cut and finely shred chicken breasts. Arrange shredded lettuce on a large flat platter. Top with shredded chicken, shallots and coriander leaves. Combine dressing ingredients in a screw-top jar and shake well. Pour over chicken and lettuce before serving. Sprinkle with toasted almond slivers. Serves 4.

Shallot Brush

A fresh crunchy garnish for the salad or cold meat platter. Using a sharp knife cut off roots and leaves. Lay the shallot down and carefully slice the light green part into thin slivers for about two thirds of the length. Soak the shallot in ice-cold water to curl the slivers.

The Tang of Chives

Chives *(Allium schoenoprasum)* are grown entirely for their leaves, which are used for flavouring in all kinds of dishes. They have been cultivated for centuries and have changed very little over the years. It is thought that they spread through the northern hemisphere from a north Russian origin. Chives have been widely used in French cooking, for sauces and salads, since the 17th century.

The chive is a well-known member of the herb garden. It is a perennial plant to 25 cm high with narrow, cylindrical and hollow leaves which have a subtle, onion-like flavour. The small mauve flowers are numerous and have a light fragrance. Bunches of chives are available in fruit markets all year round, with the main flush in summer. They are extremely easy to grow either in the garden or in pots near to the kitchen, where they will be ready to be snipped to dress up everyday meals.

To keep the plants bushy and the leaves tender, cut a few of the leaves low down on the plant rather than bobbing the top, which will brown where cut. The plant needs to be cut regularly to keep the leaves from becoming too sparse. The more it is cut, the better it will flourish and continue without loss of energy until late autumn.

Chives contain iron, pectin, calcium, sulphur and a mild natural antibiotic. In large quantities they are a source of vitamin C.

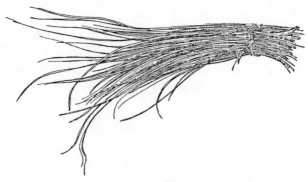

Chives

Garlic chives

Chives in the Kitchen

The flavour of chives is lost with prolonged cooking and should be cut and added to hot or cold food just before serving. Chives have an affinity with eggs and cream. They are delicious with scrambled eggs and omelettes and, combined with sour cream, make an excellent and time-honoured garnish for potatoes baked in their jackets. They go well with cream cheese, fish, chicken and mayonnaise. When chopped fine they make an attractive garnish, as an alternative to parsley, for sprinkling on soups and salads. The mauve flowers also are edible and can be added to salads, either whole or pulled apart.

Storage

Chives are best used shortly after picking. They can be kept for a short while in the refrigerator, and will remain crispy fresh when wrapped in a paper towel and placed in a plastic bag or container.

Chives do not retain their flavour well when dried, but do freeze well. They produce very little extra foliage during the winter months. In late summer when growth is lush the leaves may be chopped and placed in an ice-cube tray with a little water and quickly frozen. When frozen, tip cubes into a plastic bag or container and store in the freezer until needed.

Chive Cream

150 ml double cream
2 tablespoons finely chopped chives
juice of half a lemon
¼ teaspoon finely grated zest of lemon

Whisk the cream with the chives until stiff. Fold in the strained lemon juice and lemon zest. Gently heat the cream until warm and of pouring consistency.

Chive Butter

125 g butter, softened
2 tablespoons finely chopped chives
a squeeze of lemon juice
little salt and freshly milled pepper

Blend the butter with the chives and the lemon juice. Season with salt and pepper to taste. Form into a log shape and chill until firm. Slice and use as required. Serve with hot rolls, baked potatoes, steamed carrots and cauliflower. Chive and other herb butters should be used within a week or may be frozen for up to three months.

Lime and Chive Butter

A delicious and easy stuffing for baked fish. Save a little of the butter for melting and brushing over the fish and lightly sprinkle with dry breadcrumbs.

150 g butter, softened
1 tablespoon chives, chopped
juice and finely grated zest of 1 lime

Blend the butter with the juice and zest of the lime. Fold the chives through the butter.

Snow Peas with Lettuce and Chives

225 g snow peas
45 g butter
½ small lettuce, shredded
1 tablespoon chives, finely chopped
2 shallots, finely sliced
pinch of sugar
pinch of salt
mint leaves for garnish

Top and tail snow peas. Reserve a teaspoon of butter and melt the rest in a pan and stir in the snow peas. Add the sugar and salt and cover the pan. Cook over moderate heat for 5 minutes. Stir in the lettuce, chives and shallots. Quickly but gently toss until the lettuce has wilted. Add the remaining butter and when melted serve immediately with a garnish of mint leaves. Serves 4 as a side dish.

Chive and Onion Sticks

15 g butter
½ cup chopped chives
1 medium onion, finely chopped
2 sheets pre-rolled puff pastry
1 tablespoon milk
½ cup tasty cheese, grated

Melt butter over medium heat and add onion, stirring for about 2 minutes until onion is soft. Drain on absorbent paper and allow to cool. Mix together onion and chives and spread evenly over 1 sheet of pastry. Cover with remaining sheet. Brush with milk and sprinkle with cheese. Cut pastry into 2 cm wide strips. Twist strips and place onto greased oven trays. Brush lightly with milk. Bake in hot oven for about 8 minutes or until golden brown. Serve warm. Makes 10 to 12 sticks.

Potato Pancakes with Chives

These crisp, lacy pancakes are found in one form or another all over Europe. Serve as an accompaniment to roast or grilled meat.

4 medium potatoes, peeled and coarsely grated
2 tablespoons chives, chopped
2 teaspoons salt
black pepper, freshly ground
1 tablespoon butter
2 tablespoons oil

Place grated potatoes in mixing bowl. Add the chives, salt and pepper and mix well. Heat butter and oil in frying pan over a high heat. When foam subsides, put tablespoons of the mixture in the pan, making three or four flat heaps. Cook until golden brown on both sides. Drain well and serve immediately. Serves 4.

Variation: One tablespoon of finely chopped parsley and a crushed clove of garlic can be substituted for the chives.

Garlic Chives

Garlic chives (*Allium tuberosum*) are also known as Chinese chives or Cantonese onion. The plant is widespread in eastern Asia where it has been cultivated and used for at least two thousands years in China. The Emperor Charlemagne listed it among the 70 herbs in his garden. It grows wild in Assam in the north-east India, but there is no certainty that this is its place of origin. It is a popular herb in Japan, China, India, Nepal, Thailand and the Philippines, where both the leaves and the flowers, harvested in bud, are used in cooking.

The garlic chive is a bigger plant than the European chive and forms dense clumps of long, narrow, flat leaves to 40 cm long. The leaves have the spicy flavour of ordinary chives with just a hint of garlic. The flower-stems are angular and carry a many-flowered umbel of white starry flowers. The flowers have a pleasant heliotrope-like fragrance.

When used in large amounts the leaves of garlic chives are a source of vitamin C and carotene (vitamin A). Seeds are used in China as a tonic and for heart complaints.

Garlic Chives in the Kitchen

Wash the leaves well and pat dry. Use finely chopped in soups, omelettes and as a flavouring for stir-fry dishes or raw in salads or as a garnish. They give all noodle dishes a tangy lift. The flowers are edible and may be sprinkled in salads.

Storage

Garlic chives are sold fresh by the bunch and are easily grown. They are best when used immediately after cutting and can be stored in the same way as the European chive.

Chicken and Garlic Chives

2 chicken breasts, cut into thin shreds
½ bunch garlic chives, cut into 5 cm lengths
1 egg white
1 tablespoon cornflour
½ cup chicken stock
2 tablespoons rice wine or dry sherry
1 tablespoon soy sauce

Mix together egg white and cornflour. Combine with shredded chicken in a bowl and leave for 30 minutes. Heat oil in wok and stir-fry chicken until it turns white. Push to one side and quickly stir-fry garlic chives. Pour in chicken stock and dry sherry. Combine with the chicken and stir until the sauce thickens. Serve immediately. Serves 2 or more as part of a meal.

Roast Duck and Garlic Chives

This light and easy stir-fry recipe may be made with leftover roast duck that has been roasted at home, Chinese restaurant or bought in a Chinese market.

½ roast duck (skin optional)
3 cups garlic chives, cut into 5 cm lengths
1 cup bamboo shoots, shredded
2 tablespoons oil
2 tablespoons light soy sauce
2 teaspoons sugar

Shred the duck into linear lengths to make up about 2 cups. Heat oil in wok and stir-fry duck for about 1 minute. Add the soy sauce and half the sugar. Stir and combine with the duck for no more than a minute. Remove the duck and set aside. Add the bamboo shoots, stir briskly and then add the chives and stir to combine. Add the remaining sugar, stir through. Return the duck to the wok. Toss until thoroughly blended and hot. Serve immediately. Serves 2 or more as part of a meal.

Eccentric Onions

Rocambole

Rocambole *(Allium scorodoprasum)* gets its common name from the Danish *rocken bolle* which means 'rock onion'. It grows wild over most of Europe, western USSR and Asia Minor. It is believed that its widely scattered distribution is probably a result of its former cultivation as a culinary plant. Rocambole is now not often cultivated and is mostly collected locally in the wild. The purple garlic-like bulbs are strongly flavoured and are used for the same purposes as those of garlic. It is a larger plant than the garlic, up to 1 m high, and has flat glaucous leaves and a spirally twisted central stem. A pointed bud unwinds to reveal an umbel of small bulblets interspersed with a few light purple flowers. The edible aerial bulbs that bunch at the top are very similar in taste and form to the garlic.

Rocambole is also known as sand leek, but this common name is best applied to *A. ampeloprasum*, which grows wild in sandy soils primarily in the Mediterranean region. Botanists claim that the cultivated leek, *A. porrum* is probably derived from *A. ampeloprasum*.

The Tree Onion

The tree onion *(Allium cepa* var. *viviparum)* is also known as the Egyptian onion, which is misleading for it is unlikely that it originated in Egypt. It is a perennial that produces underground bulbs as well as clusters of small, red bulblets at the top of the flower stalk. These often germinate producing miniature onion plants on

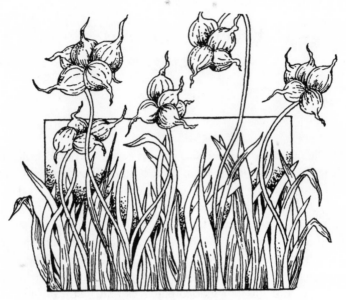

top. Because of this peculiar characteristic, it is called *kitsune negi* in Japan which means 'foxy' or 'mysterious onion'.

Production of bulblets may take place in the first or second year and they can be picked off the stems when needed. They are mild-flavoured and are excellent for pickling. Young plants are used as green onions to season soups and salads. The ripening stalks may be stuffed like celery sticks.

Onions

True shallots

Spring onions

Japanese bunching onions (shallots)

Cultivation

Onions

Every garden of any considerable size should have an onion patch simply because we use them almost every day. To ensure a continuous supply, it is a good idea to grow three or more varieties. The old saying 'he sure knows his onions' probably came from the fact that it is important for the grower to choose the right variety of onions for the right planting time. The growth of onion bulbs is controlled by the length of day, and it is therefore advisable to choose varieties and sowing times suitable to your district.

In temperate and semi-tropical climates, most varieties of onions are sown from mid-autumn to mid-winter. The early salad or bunching types, such as 'Early Barletta' and 'White Rocket', are usually sown a little earlier; around February and March.

Early maturing globe-types including 'Crystal Grano', 'Early Flat White', and 'Early Lockyer White', are usually sown in April. In general, early maturing types do not store well over long periods.

Maincrop and mid-season varieties include 'Australian Brown', 'Hunter River Brown', 'White Globe', 'Creamgold' and 'Odourless' which is a flat, mild-flavoured onion. These should be sown in early winter ready for lifting during summer.

Late maturing varieties include the large 'Prizetaker', 'Ailsa Craig' and 'White Sweet Spanish'. All have globe-shaped bulbs with a mild flavour. These should be sown in July and August, or a little later in cool climates.

Small white onions, for pickling or stews, such as 'White Queen', 'White Lisbon' or 'Silverskin' can be sown almost any time of the year and harvested when needed.

Generally seed should be sown in single rows. Place a complete fertiliser in the row and lightly cover and work in the topsoil. Sow the seed thinly in shallow furrows about 1 cm deep. In a very light soil, plant a little deeper to prevent drying. Cover with a fine compost and water gently. Germination occurs in ten to fourteen days. When seedlings emerge thin out to stand 7 to 10 cm apart. Overcrowding produces small bulbs. Seedlings from thinnings may be used for salads or like chives in cooking.

If transplanting seedlings, use plants about 15 cm high. Space them in the garden bed up to 10 cm apart in rows that are up to 30 cm apart. Ensure that only the root and bulbous portion of the stem are inserted in the soil. If planted deeper the plants do not bulb freely.

Onions must have good drainage, but need a large amount of moisture. The onion bulb prefers to sit on the soil surface, so do not hill up the soil around it. Since the roots are comparatively shallow, hand weeding will be necessary around the plants.

Onions take six to nine months to mature. Bulbs become mature after the tops have begun to fall over, due to drying in the neck region of the leaves. After lifting the bulbs, leave for a few days in the sun until the outside skin of the bulb dries out. Screw off the tops and rub off old roots. Store in well-ventilated baskets or

mesh bags in a cool, dry place. Small onions may be plaited like garlic and stored by hanging the strings.

Garlic

Garlic is easily grown from the individual cloves of the compound bulb. The outer ones are the best for planting.

There are two main types of garlic available. The variety known as Giant Russian or Jumbo is very much larger and milder than the more potent small or common garlic.

The cloves are best planted in autumn or early winter. These should be covered with about 6 cm of soil and spaced about 5 cm apart. Garlic will flourish best in a rich organic soil in a sunny position. Good drainage is important. Keep the area free of weeds and keep up the mulch if the weather is dry and hot.

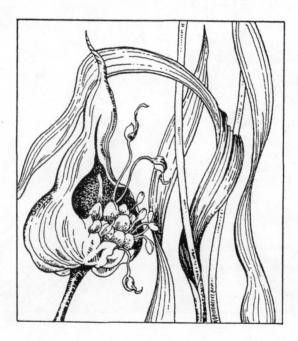

Garlic can take up to five or six months to mature. Tall flower stalks sometimes arise bearing rounded heads of tiny, pinkish-white blossoms. Seeds are rarely produced.

Harvest garlic when the leaves have turned yellow and fallen over. After harvesting, spread the bulbs out in a shady, dry situation to dry off and harden thoroughly. Tops and roots may be removed, leaving 2 cm of top, and garlic stored in open mesh bags. Alternatively, the tops may be plaited together and the strings hung in a cool, well-ventilated place ready for use. Properly dried, garlic will keep for several months.

Leeks

Leeks are troublefree and a very worthwhile vegetable to grow. They are adaptable to most climates and may be grown and harvested over a long period of time. They are, however, slow growers and may take up to 24 weeks or more to mature. They crop over a period of about 12 weeks. You can eat them while they are small though and these can be harvested any time after they are 1 cm thick.

They grow best in a rich, friable soil with a pH 6 or higher and containing an abundance of organic matter. They need plenty of moisture, especially early in their growth, but must have very good drainage. Soil should be weed-free. Feeding is important and unless the soil is very rich, leeks will respond to side dressings of nitrogen fertiliser or liquid feeds during the growing period.

Seedlings are ready to transplant when they are about 20 cm tall. To reduce transpiration, cut back the tops by about a third to one half.

Leeks are grown for their elongated, thickened stem rather than a bulb. The stems are blanched by excluding sunlight. This ensures that they grow long and white. Several methods of cultivation are used to blanch the stems.

An easy method is to plant each seedling in a hole about 15 cm deep at about 10 to 15 cm apart. A gentle watering will wash enough soil into the hole to cover the roots. Later, normal erosion and successive waterings will gradually fill the hole with soil and blanch the stems.

Alternatively, seedlings can be planted in the bottom of a compost-enriched trench about 20 cm deep, and the trench filled in gradually as the plants grow. If soil is not well drained, omit the trench and plant on the level of the soil. Mulch continuously as they grow. They should always be about a third covered in organic rich mulch. By the time they are mature, they should be banked with soil to the full height of the white stem.

Harvest leeks whenever you want them. Dig each plant with a long trowel because the plants grow deep and the stems may snap if pulled from the soil. Trim the leaves and roots. Leeks are best used when fresh, but will store in the refrigerator for a week or two.

True Shallots

Shallots are expensive to buy and are well worth growing as they multiply readily by natural division. A single bulb planted will produce a cluster of up to 15 distinct small bulbs in a growing season.

They are extremely hardy plants that thrive in most situations. The only requirement is that the soil temperature needs to be above $21°$ C for the cloves to be produced. Like most other members of the onion family, shallots do not like an acid soil and prefer a soil in the pH 6 to 6.5 range.

Plant individual cloves in late autumn in a sunny site. Space the cloves about 10 cm apart, covering lightly with soil. A fertile, friable soil will produce best results, especially if a light dressing of complete fertiliser is given during the growing period. Provide plenty of water during dry weather, but ensure the plants have good drainage. They need weed-free conditions.

If desired, blanching can be done on each side of the row.

Alternatively, young shallots may be pulled while green and about 6 mm in diameter and used as a mild-flavoured green onion. The chive-tasting green tops can also be used.

When grown for their mature cloves, they are left until the leaves are no longer upright and tend to fall over, but not yet turning in colour. Stop watering. This is usually about 14 to 16 weeks after planting. The bulbs should then be pulled out of the soil and, if the weather is dry, allowed to partly dry off on the ground for a couple of days. The plants should then be removed and bulbs thoroughly dried before final storage. Separate the bulbs and store in a well-ventilated, cool, dry place in trays, baskets or net bags. Inspect from time to time for any traces of mould or rot.

Japanese Bunching Onions

Also known as shallot, scallion and Welsh onion, it is the Japanese bunching onion *(Allium fistulosum)* which is the 'shallot' most widely grown in Australia. This is a mild-flavoured onion which forms a long neck rather than a bulb. It can be propagated by both seed and plant division. This species is quite adaptable to a wide range of climates and can be grown in cold areas.

Always use fresh seed. Seed should be planted thickly in rows and covered with about 6 mm of sifted soil. Rows may be around 50 cm apart. Seed may be planted in spring for a crop in late spring to early summer and again in autumn.

Shallots prefer a soil enriched with well-decomposed organic compost. Because the roots are shallow, they need good drainage, abundant moisture and must be kept weed-free. The bulbs divide repeatedly to form a cluster of bulbs. Harvesting is done by pulling out a side cluster, the rest can be left to continue dividing.

They are ready to be pulled when they are around 20 cm high and about as thick as a pencil. The outer leaves are peeled off and the inner leaves with the white stems are used.

Chives

Chives and garlic chives are hardy perennials which may be grown from seed, but are cultivated more commonly by dividing the clumps and planting the tiny oval bulbs. The best time for division is early to mid spring or autumn. If seeds are available sow in early spring or autumn to allow the plants to establish before winter. Chive seed should be planted when very fresh, because it does not remain viable for very long.

They will grow well in a variety of soils, but do best in a well-drained, friable soil containing plenty of organic matter. Chives will withstand cold and dry periods, but will certainly benefit from plenty of water during hot dry weather.

Chives will reach about 25 cm in height. They are often grown as a border plant in the garden and make a pleasant and useful edging for the herb garden, producing good contrasting tufts of foliage and attractive mauve pompom flowers. Several clumps are necessary in order to provide the kitchen with a good succession of fresh young leaves. Bulbs should be spaced about 10 cm apart because they will quickly multiply and make small clumps wherever they are planted. It is a good idea to lift and divide the clumps every two to three years to invigorate the tufts.

Windowboxes, troughs and flower pots are all attractive and suitable containers for growing chives. Use a good friable potting mix and ensure good drainage. Chives develop a rather large root system and should have a container large enough to accommodate growth.

To harvest chives, cut the leaves low down just above soil level. Do not bob the top of the leaves as this will cause browning. Frequent cutting or removal of leaves stimulates fresh bushy growth and tenderer leaves. The more you pick the more chives there will be. In cold climates they may die back in winter, but will shoot again in early spring.

Tree Onions

The tree onion differs from the others in that the root bears small bulbs underground and the tops bear bulblets in place of seed after the flowers have withered. The bulblets, although small, are extremely pungent.

The tree onion is a tall-growing perennial which makes an attractive accent plant at the back of a herb garden. The airborne bulbs are the best for planting. For best results the small clumps should not be split. Plant the bulbs in autumn in shallow drills, and cover the tops of the bulbs lightly with soil. Plant 25 to 30 cm apart.

Provide a humus-enriched soil and give the plants a good moisture-retaining mulch during summer. Within two years the plants will reach 1 m or more high. Stake so that the bulblets do not rest on the soil. The plants can be divided every three years.

Pick the bulblets off the stems as you need them. Tree onions are particularly useful for pickling and as an ingredient in salads and stews.

Natural Insecticides

With the increasing concern about the destruction of the ozone layer in the outer atmosphere, and the detrimental effect of many sprays and poisons, many people are turning to safer natural methods of dealing with pests in the garden.

The aromatic scents of the onion family will repel several unwanted insects, and when planted in company with some ornamental and food plants are reputed to be good general 'insect repellents' in the garden. The cabbage-white butterfly especially dislikes the onion scent. The onion is a particularly good companion for growing with all members of the cabbage family. Alternate rows of onions and carrots are said to repel both carrot and onion fly. Chives are also said to improve the growth and flavour of carrots.

Roses are partial to any member of the onion family and the combination of garlic and roses is now well-known as having a beneficial effect on one another. The smell of garlic also helps to keep aphids away. Garlic chives are also recommended as companion plants for roses and citrus and have a deterrent effect on certain insects, especially aphids and red spider. The brown skins of onions used as a mulch around roses bushes is reputed to give some protection against black spot.

A safe and effective way to control fruit fly is to apply garlic spray once a week about four weeks before fruit ripens or as soon as you suspect fruit fly in the area. As fruit ripens it may be necessary to increase spraying to a few times a week. Fruit flies feed for about a week before they mate and lay their eggs. If you can kill or trap them during this time you'll break the breeding cycle. Garlic pots; open tins placed in fruit trees or around the vegetable garden and containing a concentrated garlic mix, will also be effective. Garlic's great advantage is that it is completely harmless to people, birds and animals.

Garlic Spray

Crush two cloves garlic for every litre of water. Bring to the boil and allow to stand for 24 hours. Strain and, without diluting, pour into a spray container.

Oil Garlic Spray

Also effective on aphids, cabbage moth caterpillars, scale, red spider and is very effective against mosquito larvae.

Crush 30 garlic cloves and pour over 10 ml of paraffin oil. Cover and let stand for 24 hours. Then make a solution of pure soap in 500 ml of hot water. Pour over the garlic mixture, mix thoroughly, strain and when cool store in a container. Use as needed in dilutions of 1 part to 100 parts of water, or less depending on the strength required.

Garlic Pots

Crush three cloves of garlic and mix with 2 cups water. Attach wire handles to shallow open tins. Pour in garlic mixture and suspend 6 to 8 pots in each fruit tree. Top up mixture at least once a week for continuous control.

Chive Tea

A mild fungicide useful against downy mildew on pumpkins and cucumbers. Finely chop a bunch of chives and just cover with boiling water. Leave to cool. Pour into spray container.

Bibliography

Beck, S., Bertholle, L., & Child, J. *Mastering the Art of French Cooking*, Vols 1 & 2. Penguin Books Ltd, Middlesex, England, 1966.

Blackwood, J. & Fulder, S. *Garlic: Nature's Original Remedy*, Javelin Books, Dorset, 1981.

Brouk, B. *Plants Consumed by Man*, Academic Press, London, 1975.

Carrier, R. *Great Dishes of the World*, Thomas Nelson & Sons Ltd, 1963.

David, E. *A Book of Mediterranean Food*, Revised Edn. Penguin Books Ltd, Middlesex, England, 1965.

David, E. *French Provincial Cooking*, Penguin Books Ltd, Middlesex, England, 1964.

Grieve, M.P. *A Modern Herbal*, Penguin Books Ltd, Middlesex, England, 1974.

Grigson, J. *Good Things*, Penguin Books Ltd, Middlesex, England, 1973.

Grigson, J. *Vegetable Book*, Penguin Books Ltd, Middlesex, England, 1979.

Hazan, M.P. *The Classic Italian Cookbook*, Papermac, London, 1981.

Herklots, G.A.C. *Vegetables in South-East Asia*, London, 1972.

Moore, H.E. Jr. *The Cultivated Alliums*, Vols. 2. Baileya, 1954.

Stearn, W.T. *European species of Allium and allied genera of Alliaceae:* Ann. Musei Goulandris 4: 83–198. 1978.

Usher, G. *A Dictionary of Plants Used by Man*, Constable and Company Ltd. London, 1974.

Yamaguchi, M. *World Vegetables*, The AVI Publishing Company, Inc., Connecticut, 1983.

Recipe Index